GREEN TECH

ECO-FRIENDLY LIVING

KATIE DICKER

WAYLAND

First published in Great Britain in 2021 by Wayland

Copyright © Hodder and Stoughton Limited, 2021

 Produced for Wayland by
White-Thomson Publishing Ltd
www.wtpub.co.uk

Editor: Katie Dicker
Series Designer: Rocket Design (East Anglia) Ltd
Consultant: Dr Sharon George

HB ISBN: 978 1 5263 1524 3
PB ISBN: 978 1 5263 1525 0

Wayland
An imprint of
Hachette Children's Group
Part of Hodder & Stoughton
Carmelite House
50 Victoria Embankment
London EC4Y 0DZ

An Hachette UK Company
www.hachettechildrens.co.uk

Printed in China

Picture acknowledgements:
Alamy: Kevin Britland / Alamy Stock Photo 7b; American Chemical Society 21b; Blue Planet Ltd reference for 9b; Cambridge Consultants 22bl and 31; Getty: Abscent84 3t and 23tr, Medesulda 3b and 24m, bagrovskam 4, IngaNielsen 5b, DrAfter123 6, sompong_tom 16t, Youst 17, Goran13 19bl, Jason Finn 25t, elenabs 26–27b and 32, Tempura 27t, Pixtum 28t, Jon Wightman 28b; ©MIT/AMS Institute 27br; Shutterstock: SkyPics Studio cover tl, title bl and 10–11, petovarga cover tr, title tr, 24b and 30b, metamorworks cover ml, 7t and 26m, Mary Long cover m and title tl, Yauhen 44 cover mr, Lucky clover cover bl, Evgenia.B cover bm, Macrovector cover br, title br and 14, Siberian Art 2 and 21t, laymanzoom 5t, pathdoc 8, Zakharchenko Anna 11t, Boris Bulychev 12b, vectortatu 12ml, Mascha Tace 12mr, Vectorpocket 13t, Sketchbook Designs 15tr, Borisovstudio 15b, jossnat 16b, extripod 18m, Julia Tim 19tr, Lemberg Vector studio 20, Oceloti 23b, shaineast 25b, Abugrafie 29t; Smart Cups 18bl; University of Colorado Boulder College of Engineering and Applied Science 9t; WTE Ltd reference for 13b; www.collectors2020.eu reference for 19br; www.sdwforall.com 29b.

All design elements from Shutterstock or drawn by designer.

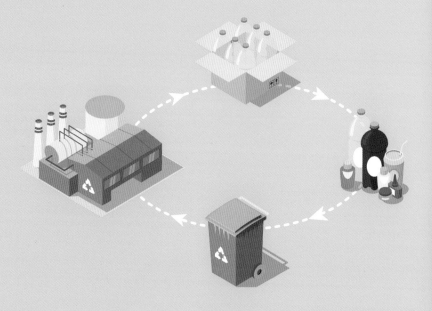

CONTENTS

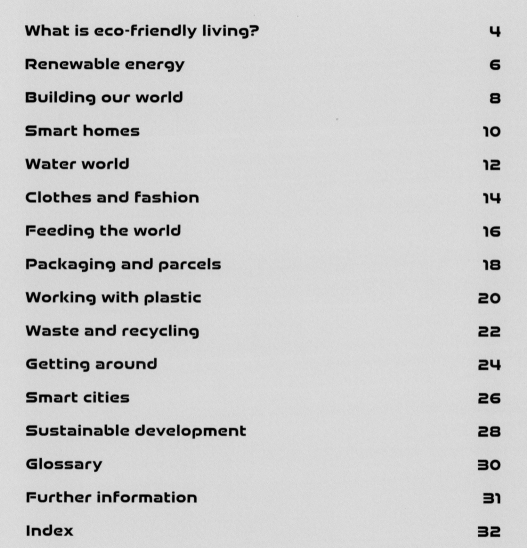

WHAT IS ECO-FRIENDLY LIVING?

Every day, the world's population grows by over 200,000 people and we're using more resources than ever before. Our activities are causing Earth's climate to get dangerously warmer. To limit our impact on Earth, we need to make some changes.

LOOKING AHEAD

For a long time, we didn't know quite how much damage we were causing and the consequences of the way we used Earth's resources. But when scientists noticed changes in Earth's climate, it became clear we had a serious problem. The gradual rise in Earth's temperature is putting our planet and the life within it at risk. We are polluting our environment and slowly running out of natural resources.

Planet Earth has the right conditions for life, but its future is in our hands.

PROTECTING EARTH

Eco-friendly living is about reducing the impact we have on our planet. It is something we can all do – from the food we eat to the clothes we wear, and the way we travel around. Governments play an important part, too. Regulations ensure that new buildings are designed to be eco-friendly for example (see page 8), and improved public transport helps to reduce pollution.

Earth Overshoot Day

Earth Overshoot Day is the day we use up a year's worth of natural resources (the amount that Earth can regenerate in a year). In 1970, it was 29 December. In 2019, it was 29 July! We can't go on like this forever.

POWERFUL TECH

If we all make changes in our own lives, together we can make a big difference. Thankfully, some amazing technology is helping to speed up the process. Green tech has provided ways to use Earth's resources more efficiently. It has opened up non-polluting sources of energy and is helping poorer parts of the world to develop in an eco-friendly way. But it's also important that we continue to protect our natural world, rather than relying on technology to clean up our mess.

RENEWABLE ENERGY

For many years, we've used non-renewable resources to produce energy. Fossil fuels such as coal and oil, for example, will eventually run out. They also create harmful gases when they're burned. Scientists have developed renewable sources of energy that are cleaner and won't run out.

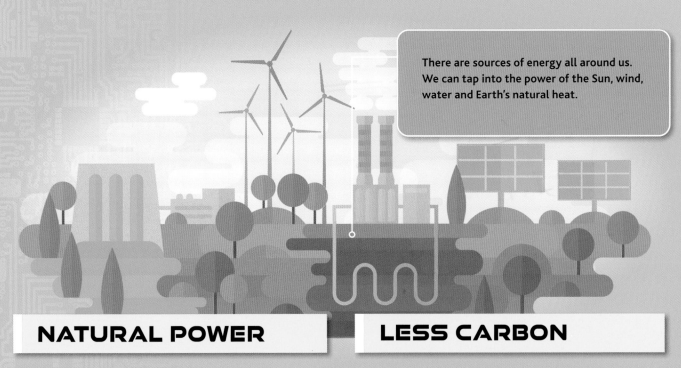

There are sources of energy all around us. We can tap into the power of the Sun, wind, water and Earth's natural heat.

NATURAL POWER

Renewable sources of energy use the power of nature. For example, the strength of the wind or of flowing water can turn a turbine to spin a generator and create electricity. The energy in sunlight can be captured to heat and power our homes. Earth's natural heat can warm water, and plant or animal waste can be used for fuel.

LESS CARBON

Scientists talk about carbon emissions or our 'carbon footprint' (the amount of carbon produced by an activity). This refers mainly to 'carbon dioxide' but also includes other greenhouse gases that warm our planet. An increase of these gases in our atmosphere traps more of the Sun's heat than is healthy for Earth. Renewable energy reduces this growing pollution and preserves resources.

CHANGING BEHAVIOUR

It can be difficult to change people's behaviour, but knowledge is often the key. Technology can now monitor our 'personal carbon footprint', for example, to find out the impact of the energy we're using. This knowledge can help us to make small changes to our lifestyles, creating new habits that bring us benefits (such as saving money) while also helping to save the planet.

Knowing our energy use can help us to make informed choices about our daily activities.

DID YOU KNOW?

The Sun's energy can now be used to power ovens, run air conditioning units, power streetlights and charge electronic devices. Scientists are currently developing cars that use solar power to recharge their batteries.

SOLAR POWER

As technology improves, it becomes easier to make changes at home, especially when governments subsidise eco-friendly tech (that is, make it cheaper for people to buy). For example, many more homes in the USA, Germany and Italy now use solar panels on roofs and in glass 'solar panel' skylights. Energy and resources are needed to make solar panels, but once in place, they can power homes and other buildings in sunny climates.

New roofs can be made from 'solar shingle tiles' – small solar panels that look like traditional roof tiles.

BUILDING OUR WORLD

We all need houses and places to work, but we need to reduce the impact that new buildings have on our planet. Manufacturing building materials, transporting them to building sites and the construction process itself, produces nearly 11 per cent of annual carbon emissions.

FEWER EMISSIONS

The construction of eco-friendly buildings produces fewer polluting gases. Instead of using cement and steel, wood has become a popular choice (and is long-lasting if well maintained). Trees absorb carbon dioxide from the air and store it safely in their trunks, so sustainable forests can reduce greenhouse gases while also providing a useful building material. If wood is grown locally, less fuel is needed to transport it.

DID YOU KNOW?

Wood absorbs approximately 1 tonne of carbon dioxide per cubic metre of wood – an average wooden family house could store the carbon one family produces by driving their car for ten years!

LIVING MATERIALS

Scientists have been looking at other biological building materials, ones that are still 'living'! They have found that under the right conditions, bacteria absorb carbon dioxide as they grow, to make a cement-like material. Although humid conditions are needed to stop the bacteria drying out, scientists think these bacteria-bricks could one day heal their own cracks as they age!

Living concrete can be 'grown' in a laboratory and moulded into different shapes.

LOCAL SOLUTIONS

Scientists are also using emissions from local power plants to create a form of limestone. By taking the flue gases and bubbling them through salty water, the carbon dioxide (CO_2) combines with calcium from waste concrete to create calcium carbonate ($CaCO_3$) or limestone. The limestone rocks can then be used in new concrete. This method cuts down power plant emissions, but also reduces the mining and transportation of natural limestone.

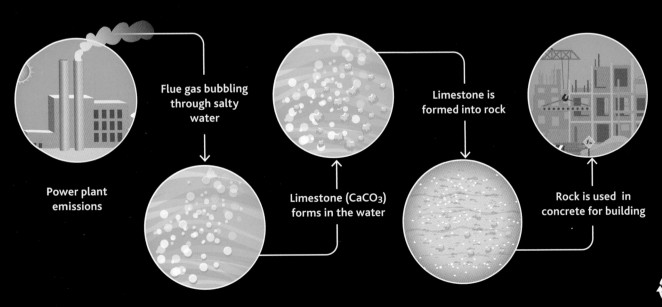

Power plant emissions

Flue gas bubbling through salty water

Limestone ($CaCO_3$) forms in the water

Limestone is formed into rock

Rock is used in concrete for building

 SMART HOMES

Once our homes and workplaces are built, we need energy to light, power, heat and cool them. This energy produces about 20 per cent of the world's carbon emissions, although lifestyle changes and technology are helping to lower this figure.

EFFICIENT LIGHTING

New types of light bulbs have helped to cut our energy use. LED lights, for example, use up to 80 per cent less energy than older incandescent bulbs. Smart sensors can help to make even more savings (see diagram below).

HEAT AND POWER

Smart technology can also control our heating and power supplies (see diagram). Monitors can show the energy use and costs of individual appliances, with tips on how to make savings.

 Energy management system monitors and controls the power consumption of lights, appliances, heating and air conditioning.

 Lights are programmed to switch on when it gets dark (or when someone enters a room), and their brightness can be controlled individually.

 Smart air conditioning works when the background temperature rises. It switches off when a window opens or if no one is at home.

SAVING ENERGY

Did you know that some electronic devices use 'phantom power' when they're turned off but still plugged into a socket? These include gadgets that use a remote control or those, such as microwaves, with a continuous digital clock display. You can save this energy by using a 'smart power strip' – this cuts the power supply if a device is left on standby, or when a device has finished charging.

Phantom power

The average home has 40 products that constantly use power. These make up at least 10 per cent of a household's energy use – energy that could be saved.

Smart thermostats turn the heating on when the background temperature falls. Smart radiator valves know which rooms aren't used regularly.

Smart appliances turn 'off' when they're not in use and 'on' at particular times when there's plenty of energy going spare.

Smart bathroom appliances keep water flow and temperature at preferred settings.

SUPPLY AND DEMAND

Scientists are also using computer data to predict our behaviour. This 'artificial intelligence' can learn our daily routine. Instead of a constant supply, power can be produced to meet demand at certain times of day, generating fewer carbon emissions.

WATER WORLD

Earth's water cycle moves a constant supply of water, but we're using more water than ever, and can't create any more! Less than 3 per cent of Earth's water is fresh (not salty), and this isn't always accessible. Water has to be treated so we can use it to drink, cook, wash and make different products.

SAVING WATER

You'd be surprised how much water it takes to have a shower or run a bath. Smart meters encourage us to use less water at home, but it's important to remember that everything we eat, use, buy and wear also has a 'water footprint'. It takes about 125 litres of water to produce a single apple, for example.

An average bath uses 80 litres of water, while an eight-minute shower uses 60 litres.

MODERN APPLIANCES

In richer countries, the use of modern appliances such as dishwashers has increased average water use. Thankfully, green tech is helping to reduce the amount of water we use each day. Studies have shown that the latest dishwashers, for example, now use less water and energy than the 'running tap' method of washing up, which uses a steady stream of hot water.

Think twice before you wash and rinse!

SELF-CLEANING CLOTHES

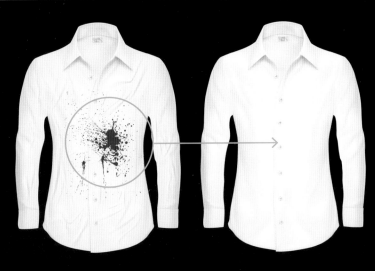

Science is helping to find new ways to keep our clothes clean.

To address the amount of water we're using to clean our clothes (a washing machine uses 50 litres per average wash), scientists have been developing textiles that clean themselves! They found that fabric covered with a thin layer of titanium oxide particles releases electrons when exposed to sunlight or artificial light. The electrons combine with oxygen molecules, enabling them to break down dirt and stains. The challenge now is to make this technology suitable for mass production.

Use at home

Toilet flushes use the most water at home. The average person flushes the toilet over 1,500 times a year!

- clothes washing — 13%
- showers — 12%
- baths and taps — 21%
- other — 5%
- drinking water — 4%
- washing up — 8%
- outdoor — 7%
- toilet flushing — 30%

DETECTING LEAKS

Around the world, more than 45 million cubic metres of water are lost every day due to faulty plumbing and leaky pipes. Scientists have been working on real-time leakage detection systems that raise the alarm as soon as a problem occurs. The water supply can be switched off remotely, preventing further loss until the problem is fixed.

CLOTHES AND FASHION

Many people throw away old clothes or buy things they never really wear – shopping habits that harm our planet. Textile production uses nearly 80 billion cubic metres of fresh water and releases 1.2 billion tonnes of carbon emissions a year, as well as transport and other costs.

FAST FASHION

Recent years have seen an increase in clothes consumption known as 'fast fashion'. Cheap clothes based on the latest trends are worn a few times until the fashion changes again. To slow things down, we need to change this behaviour. Buying fewer clothes that are longer-lasting (or buying second-hand clothes) reduces the need for new materials. It's better to mend clothes and to recycle things that can't be worn again. Sharing, swapping or renting clothes is also becoming more popular.

The clothing industry releases more than 10 per cent of the world's carbon emissions each year.

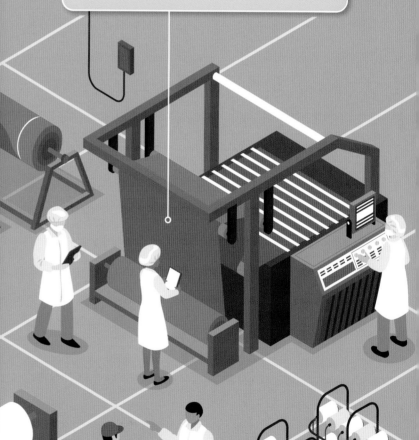

DIFFERENT FABRICS

Producing artificial fabrics (such as polyester) uses more energy than producing plant-based fibres (such as hemp). Artificial fabrics aren't biodegradable because they're a type of plastic (see page 20), and some contain microfibres that pollute water when they're washed. Scientists have been developing more eco-friendly fibres, such as tencel. Reusing the water and chemicals needed to extract them also saves on water and reduces pollution.

Tencel is a new fabric that comes from the eucalyptus tree, which can be grown in sustainable forests.

LIVE ORGANISMS

Scientists are also developing strong, flexible fibres from live organisms, such as bacteria, yeast and fungi! These biodegradable materials could be grown on smaller areas of land without using pesticides. They could also be grown to fit moulds, so less 'off-cut' material goes to waste. Scientists think the fabrics could even repair their own rips or tears!

DID YOU KNOW?

Over 500,000 tonnes of microfibres reach the oceans each year – the equivalent of more than 50 billion plastic bottles.

This laser machine cuts fabrics, but waste material is left behind. New fabrics could be grown to exact shapes.

FEEDING THE WORLD

We have over 7 billion people to feed, but a rich minority use far more food resources than the rest. Food production uses about 30 per cent of our energy and creates about 30 per cent of carbon emissions. It also uses a lot of fresh water and land.

CITY FARMS

As Earth's climate warms, our crops are at risk. 'Indoor vertical farms' are one way to create a sustainable food supply in cities. By stacking plants on top of each other in a controlled environment, these farms produce crops in a limited space, and avoid transportation costs to another location because they feed city residents. They also use up to 70 per cent less water than traditional farms.

Could vertical farms be the food of the future for city dwellers?

SMART EQUIPMENT

Drones and sensors can monitor soil conditions on a large traditional farm and find diseased or damaged crops. Robots and automated tractors can help with planting, watering and harvesting. The use of data and artificial intelligence can also help farmers to predict future conditions and grow crops more successfully.

SHOPPING HABITS

Meat and dairy farming use over 80 per cent of the world's farmland and create 60 per cent of agriculture's emissions (cows produce a lot of methane, for example, mainly through belching!). We can help by eating more plant-based foods. Local, seasonal foods (that don't require heated greenhouses) have no need to be transported. Apps can help shoppers to make smarter choices, using data from food labels or shopping receipts to estimate the environmental impact of different foods.

It takes 5,000–20,000 litres of water to produce 1 kg of meat.

FOOD WASTE

About a third of the food we produce is currently wasted (or lost through spoilage). If food waste enters landfill, it releases harmful methane (see page 23). We can reduce waste by watching out for sell-by dates and only buying or serving what we need. Technology can also make our supply systems more efficient. For example, new apps advertise leftover food from shops and restaurants or 'imperfect' produce such as wonky fruit and vegetables, to be sold at a reduced price.

DID YOU KNOW?

If every week, families in the UK changed one red-meat-based meal for a plant-based meal, over the course of a year it would reduce the same carbon footprint as taking 16 million cars off the road!

PACKAGING AND PARCELS

Our food is packaged to stay fresh, our toiletries come in bottles and cans, and we're shopping online more than ever. Packaging needs to be reusable to save Earth's resources. We can all use a 'bag for life' or a reusable coffee cup, but can we do more?

PLANT-BASED MATERIALS

Most packaging, such as cardboard, can be recycled. But recycling uses a lot of energy (see page 22). Suppliers are turning to biodegradable packaging made from plant-based fibres. Sugarcane and coconut husks can be used for packaging and cartons (see right), and mushroom-based packaging used to protect delicate goods.

EDIBLE PACKAGING

To help reduce waste, some packaging can now be eaten or composted. For example, sweet or cupcake wrappers made from rice or potato starch, dissolvable sachets made from seaweed, and party cups made from a seaweed-based gelatin that taste like jelly! Adding ingredients to packaging (see left) is another way to reduce the materials we use, if the packaging is composted in the correct manner.

Ingredients are printed in the packaging of this compostable plant-based cup so you just add water to make an energy drink.

DRONE DELIVERIES

An increase in online shopping has meant more home deliveries, raising fuel consumption and carbon emissions. In the future, robots or drones could deliver our packages for us. While drones are currently good at getting supplies to remote areas, scientists are looking at ways to improve the cost, safety, security and accuracy of delivering packages in busy cities.

Drone deliveries could reduce transportation costs, but more research is needed into their safety and security.

SMART SOLUTIONS

To cut down on food waste (see page 17), smart packaging can record more reliable 'best before' dates so food isn't wasted unnecessarily. One designer has proposed a gel-filled label that starts to create bumps on the packaging when the food inside becomes unsafe to eat. Plastic labels on fruit and vegetables can also be replaced with laser technology that harmlessly marks the skin.

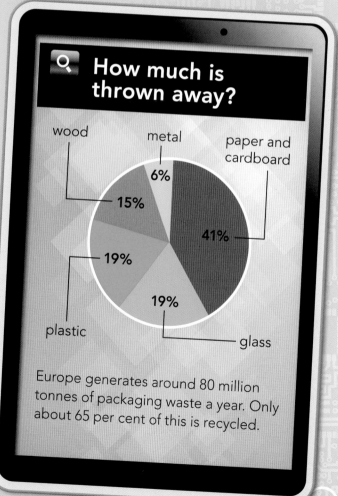

How much is thrown away?

- wood
- metal
- paper and cardboard — 41%
- 6%
- 15%
- 19% — plastic
- 19% — glass

Europe generates around 80 million tonnes of packaging waste a year. Only about 65 per cent of this is recycled.

WORKING WITH PLASTIC

Plastic is a hot topic and companies worldwide are trying to reduce the amount of plastic in their packaging. Using plastic is a hygienic way to keep food fresher for longer, but it doesn't break down when thrown away and is polluting our land and oceans.

There are an estimated 17,760 pieces of plastic in every square kilometre of ocean.

SAFER RECYCLING

Many plastics can be recycled using chemicals, machines or heat. But these processes use a lot of energy and cause pollution themselves. Although we can try to avoid using single-use plastics, such as straws and water bottles, we still need to deal with the plastics that have already been produced. Scientists are developing a way to use bacteria to digest plastic and turn it into an eco-friendly material that can be recycled easily or used as a building material.

DID YOU KNOW?

Since 1950, we've produced an estimated 8.3 billion tonnes of plastic, of which we have thrown away 6.3 billion tonnes! Nearly 80 per cent of this waste has ended up in landfill or has been found in our environment.

REUSABLE RESOURCES

In 2019, scientists discovered a new plastic polymer called PDK (Polydiketoenamine). They found it could be recycled again and again without losing its strength. If PDK was used for new plastic products, less plastic would need to be made.

Scientists had another breakthrough in 2019 when they realised waste plastic could be turned into chemicals and used to generate electricity. The plastic could be recycled without using fossil fuels or producing carbon emissions, although the process was only carried out on a small scale.

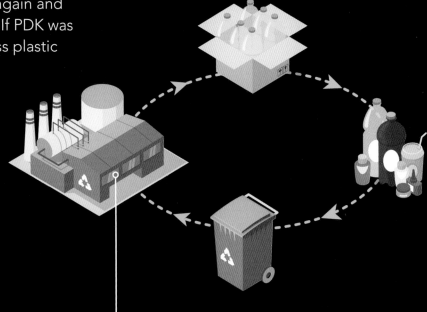

Finding more efficient ways to recycle the plastic we already have can help to reduce plastic levels in the future.

ALTERNATIVE PLASTICS

Plant-based plastics are one solution for takeaway cups and containers. These can now be made from materials such as sugar, agar (seaweed) and mycelium (found in fungi) (see page 18). Film wrapping can be made from a milk protein that is edible, printable and biodegradable. It also keeps out oxygen 500 times more efficiently than traditional plastic film.

Scientists tested their milk-protein film as packaging for blocks of cheese.

WASTE AND RECYCLING

We should always try to reduce or reuse the things we have, before recycling or throwing them away. The recycling process uses a lot of energy, as well as producing carbon emissions. Our household waste goes to landfill or is burned, causing further emissions.

SEPARATING WASTE

A new invention called the VolCat (volatile catalyst) cleans and separates materials for recycling in a hot pressurised oven, removing the need to wash and sort them first. Although VolCat uses energy, it means more complex materials can be recycled, too.

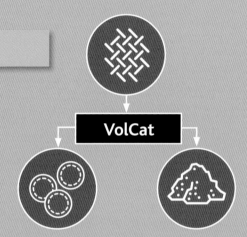

The VolCat can break down a cotton/polyester blend of fabric into a ball of cotton fibres and polyester powder.

SMART BINS

Some 'smart bins' use image recognition and artificial intelligence to identify materials and separate them for recycling. Others use solar power to compress the waste and a signal is sent when the bin needs emptying. In some countries, smart bins identify and track recycling habits, and consumers are charged a fee for un-recycled waste.

This smart recycling bin uses image recognition to light up the correct chute.

TACKLING E-WASTE

With technology developing all the time, electronic waste is a big problem. About 50 million tonnes is generated each year (the same as throwing away 1,000 laptops a second!). E-waste contains toxic chemicals, such as lead and mercury. Scientists have been finding ways to make circuit boards that dissolve in water after use, and ways to use bacteria to extract the different metals.

Our increased reliance on computers, mobile phones and smart technology means that e-waste recycling is more important than ever.

LANDFILL CLEAN-UP

Rotting waste in landfill is a source of methane emissions – a greenhouse gas 28 times more harmful than carbon dioxide. Scientists have been looking at ways to turn this methane into electricity. Tubes collect the gas, which is then compressed. The heat generated is used to boil water to power a steam turbine and generate electricity. Methane gas can also be used as a biofuel or converted into hydrogen gas to power vehicles as part of a fuel cell.

Landfills release 12 per cent of the world's methane emissions.

DID YOU KNOW?

Every year, over 2 billion tonnes of household waste is produced globally – more than 60 tonnes of waste a second! For every bag of waste, about 70 bags has been generated earlier to create the products that are now waste.

GETTING AROUND

With increased demand for global travel, as well as the import and export of different products, transport emissions are on the rise. Transport by road, rail, sea and air releases over 24 per cent of global carbon emissions, mainly to fulfil the demands of richer nations.

REDUCING EMISSIONS

Walking, cycling, car-sharing and taking public transport are good ways to reduce the number of cars on our roads and the emissions they release. Keeping a car well maintained, with properly inflated tyres can also mean it uses less fuel. For longer journeys, taking trains instead of planes is preferable. Navigation apps can now show us the 'carbon cost' of a trip, so we can make an informed choice about our journeys.

Studies show that travelling from London to Paris by train instead of plane reduces the journey's carbon emissions by 91 per cent!

GOING ELECTRIC

Electric cars could mean far lower carbon emissions, as long as their batteries are charged with renewable energy. The challenge is to make these cars more affordable and to improve their batteries. Scientists are currently working on a 'supercapacitor' that could be up to 10,000 times more powerful than existing car batteries, allowing cars to travel further between charges and fully recharge in a few minutes.

MAINTAINING ROADS

Keeping roads in good shape improves vehicles' efficiency, helping to lower emissions. Some road surfaces are now made from recycled plastic as it doesn't degrade. Studies have shown that growing trees alongside busy, populated roads can help to filter harmful particles from the air. The leaves absorb and store some of the pollution, which is then washed away by the rain.

Trees alongside a busy school road can help to absorb emissions from cars and buses.

TRAVEL AND TOURISM

It's important that we cut down on air travel, unnecessary trips and planes that fly with empty seats. In the future, planes could be powered by a newly developed jet fuel that uses industrial waste gases and lowers emissions by 50–70 per cent. Bacteria are used to turn the gases into ethanol (alcohol), which can be converted into a liquid fuel.

DID YOU KNOW?

Technology can bring a taste of tourism, without the need to travel. You can experience the sights, sounds and senses of climbing Mount Everest, for example, from the comfort of your own home, using a virtual reality headset.

SMART CITIES

Today, over 55 per cent of people worldwide live in cities, and this figure is expected to reach nearly 70 per cent by 2050. Scientists have been looking at ways to make our city spaces cleaner and less polluting, and to help city dwellers live in a more eco-friendly way.

GETTING CONNECTED

The Internet has revolutionised our world, and its uses are multiplying. 'The Internet of Things' describes the way different devices can connect to the Internet and share information. Traffic light sensors, for example, can keep traffic moving. Drivers can be alerted to their nearest parking spot or car-charging station. Waste can be collected only when the bins are nearly full. The opportunities are endless!

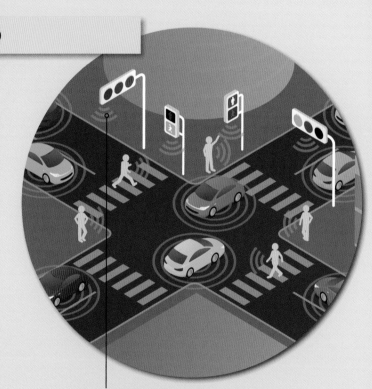

Traffic light sensors help to ease congestion, which in turn prevents the build-up of fumes.

DID YOU KNOW?

Smart-city solutions could reduce carbon emissions by up to 15 per cent, solid waste by up to 130 kg per person per year, and up to 80 litres of water per person per day.

TRANSFORMING DUBAI

Many cities around the world are striving to improve their energy efficiency and to reduce emissions. In 2013, for example, the United Arab Emirates (UAE) announced the 'Smart Dubai Initiative' to make the city more sustainable. Dubai now has electric-car charging stations, smart parking systems, traffic monitoring, smart energy meters and a smart power grid to regulate energy supplies.

CLEVER CANALS

In Amsterdam, the world's first robotic boats are being developed to transform the city and its 165 canals. These 'roboats' have cameras and sensors to collect data. If the city's streets become too busy, the boats form floating bridges or stages that can temporarily ease congestion. With satellite navigation and sensors, they can find the shortest route from A to B, and avoid traffic in their path.

Amsterdam's roboats will be used 'on-demand' to transport people and goods, and to collect waste.

SUSTAINABLE DEVELOPMENT

Poorer countries have a lower carbon footprint than richer ones, but how can they improve living standards in an eco-friendly way? Technology is helping to bridge the gap with the sharing of ideas as well as past mistakes.

PARTNERS WORLDWIDE

Richer countries have a responsibility to share knowledge with countries seeking to catch up. Technology can connect key people in an international development project, helping to combine local knowledge with hi-tech solutions, such as loaning expensive farming machinery to those in need.

RELIABLE POWER

In India, many poor rural communities don't have access to affordable, reliable electricity. Their only source of reliable power is a polluting diesel generator. A new project is aiming to build 10,000 solar microgrids to power nearly 5 million Indian homes. Each year this will cut 1 million tonnes of carbon emissions and 57 million litres of diesel.

The electricity produced by solar microgrids in India will have a huge impact on local jobs, farming, education and healthcare.

SHARING KNOWLEDGE

In Kenya and Tanzania, technology is revolutionising the lives of farmers. Rural farmers can be isolated due to poorly maintained roads and the problem of a global language barrier. Text-based services reach farmers with a mobile phone (but no Internet access). They can order seeds and fertilisers by text and any questions are answered using artificial intelligence.

For farmers with Internet access, weather updates, subtitled videos on farming techniques and access to an online marketplace are all improving efficiency.

Innovative ideas

In 2019, Anna Luísa Beserra from Brazil was named a 'Young Champion of the Earth' by the United Nations. Her idea of using the Sun's energy to kill harmful bacteria in rain water, making it safe to drink, really inspired the judges!

LAST WORD

Of course, technology isn't the only answer to our problems. The Internet uses around 10 per cent of the world's electricity consumption, for example. But it's helping us to see a way forward. So many green tech ideas have taken their inspiration from the wonders of nature – trees, rocks and bacteria that absorb carbon, and living organisms that reproduce rapidly. If we can make changes to the way we live and use technology to help us tap into Earth's natural ability to heal, there is great hope for the future.

automated something that works automatically, with minimum human input

biodegradable material that breaks down naturally into the soil or water

biofuel fuel made from plant material, animal waste or captured methane gas

carbon footprint amount of emissions released as the result of an activity

data information, facts and figures collected and used to better understand something

drone unmanned flying device that can be controlled from a distance, or using sensors and satellite navigation

electrons tiny particles charged with electrical energy, found inside small particles called atoms

emissions substances – typically harmful, polluting gases – released into the air

flue gases mixture of gases produced when a substance is burned

fossil fuel natural fuel, such as oil, that takes millions of years to form and can be burned for energy or heat

fresh water naturally occurring water that is not salty

fuel cell battery that uses the chemical energy of a fuel to produce electricity

greenhouse gas gas that traps the Sun's heat in Earth's atmosphere, warming our planet

incandescent bulb light bulb that glows when a wire inside it becomes hot

microfibres tiny artificial fibres used in some fabrics

microgrid small-scale power grid that generates electricity

molecule group of two or more small particles, called atoms, that make a particular substance

organism living thing of any kind

pesticides substances used to destroy insects or other living things that might damage crops

polymer big molecule made up of small repeating units

sustainable a way of doing things that can continue for a long time. For example, a sustainable use of Earth's resources

thermostat device that regulates the temperature of a system

FURTHER INFORMATION

BOOKS

Eco Works: How Carbon Footprints Work
by Nick Hunter (Franklin Watts)
Learn what makes up someone's carbon footprint
and what we can do to reduce it.

Putting the Planet First: Eco-cities
by Nancy Dickmann (Wayland)
From recycling drinking water to green transport links,
find out how cities are becoming more sustainable.

This Book is Not Rubbish
by Isabel Thomas (Wren & Rook)
Discover how saving the planet is not as difficult as you think.

VIDEOS

How a Family of 5 Make Almost Zero Waste
youtube.com/watch?v=B5ijPk5_8pM
The inspiring story of a waste-free family from Hobart, Australia.

Climate Friendly Living – Eco Eye series 15
youtube.com/watch?v=t_EI1FUD4Ns
Dr Lara Dungan learns about her own carbon footprint and how to
minimise its impact.

5 Eco-Friendly Building Materials
youtube.com/watch?v=NrQOZfMEXeQ
Discover how buildings of the future could change, and why LEGO®
skills are more important than you think!

INDEX

GREEN TECH

TITLES IN THE SERIES

CLEAN AND SAFE WATER
TECHNOLOGY TO SAVE OUR WORLD

- Why is clean water important?
- Water purification
- Harvesting water
- Smart controllers
- Freshwater pollution
- Saltwater desalination
- Plastic debris
- Ocean acidification
- Oil spills
- Living shorelines
- Urban solutions
- Saving water
- Basic sanitation

ECO-FRIENDLY LIVING
TECHNOLOGY TO SAVE OUR WORLD

- What is eco-friendly living?
- Renewable energy
- Building our world
- Smart homes
- Water world
- Clothes and fashion
- Feeding the world
- Packaging and parcels
- Working with plastic
- Waste and recycling
- Getting around
- Smart cities
- Sustainable development

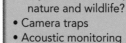

PROTECTING NATURE AND WILDLIFE
TECHNOLOGY TO SAVE OUR WORLD

- Why do we need to protect nature and wildlife?
- Camera traps
- Acoustic monitoring
- Seed banks
- DNA analysis
- Drones
- LiDAR remote sensing
- Citizen science projects
- Wildlife satellite tracking
- Wildlife crime detection
- 'Green' cities
- Pheromone traps
- Indigenous land stewarding

SOLVING THE CLIMATE CRISIS
TECHNOLOGY TO SAVE OUR WORLD

- What is the climate crisis?
- Electric and hybrid cars
- High-speed trains
- Wind power
- Solar power
- Geothermal energy and ground source heat
- Using satellites
- Extracting ice cores
- Lab-grown meat
- Climate-resistant crops
- Solar geoengineering
- Carbon capture and storage
- Reforestation and rewilding